LAUNCH INTO SPACE!

Astronauts Explore the
GALAXY

Carmen Bredeson
with
Marianne Dyson

Enslow Publishing
101 W. 23rd Street
Suite 240
New York, NY 10011
USA
enslow.com

Words to Know

astronaut—A person who works in outer space.

cosmic—Having to do with the universe.

engineering—The study of how things work.

free fall—The downward movement of an object caused by gravity pulling on it.

galaxy—A very big group of stars.

gravity—The force that pulls objects toward each other.

laboratory—A place for testing things.

orbit—To move in an oval path around a star, planet, or moon.

Contents

Awesome Astronauts

An astronaut is a person who works in outer space. Some astronauts are pilots who fly spaceships. Others study things in a laboratory. Each person has a job to do during a trip to space.

Cosmic Fact

The word *astronaut* comes from the Greek words meaning "star sailor."

Before blasting off into space, astronauts strap into their seats. Rocket engines *ROAR*! The spaceship starts to shake as it lifts off. UP it goes! About eight minutes later, the ship starts to orbit Earth.

Cosmic Fact

Astronauts may be strapped into their seats for many hours before the spaceship blasts off. They wear diapers during liftoff!

Welcome to Outer Space!

Free fall is the downward movement of an object caused by gravity pulling on it. Astronauts and objects float in space because they are falling "beside" each other like skydivers only with no air to slow them down. They stay up in space because they are going fast enough to balance the force of gravity pulling them down toward Earth.

Some astronauts visit the space station. It is a big laboratory that moves in orbit high above Earth. Scientists live there to study how objects act in space. They even study how *they* act in space!

Cosmic Fact

A spaceship can go all the way around Earth in 90 minutes.

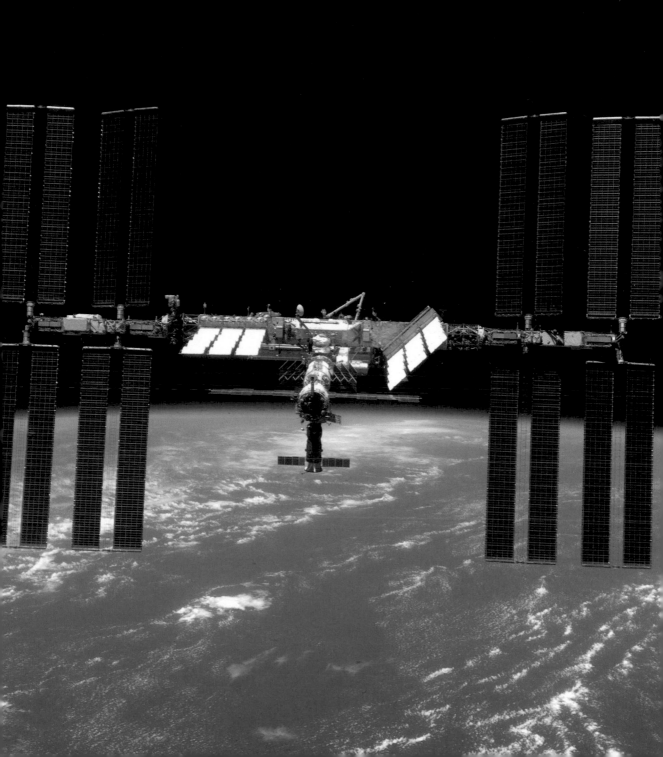

Working in Space

Astronauts have different jobs. They study how things grow in space. They also test machines that will be used on trips to the Moon or Mars. Some astronauts study whether people can stay healthy in space. Others take space walks.

Space walks are when astronauts go outside the spaceship or space station to work. Then they wear big space suits. The suits protect them from extremely hot and cold temperatures. The suits also give them air to breathe.

Cosmic Fact

Floating can make astronauts feel dizzy. Then they get used to the feeling of floating and stop feeling dizzy.

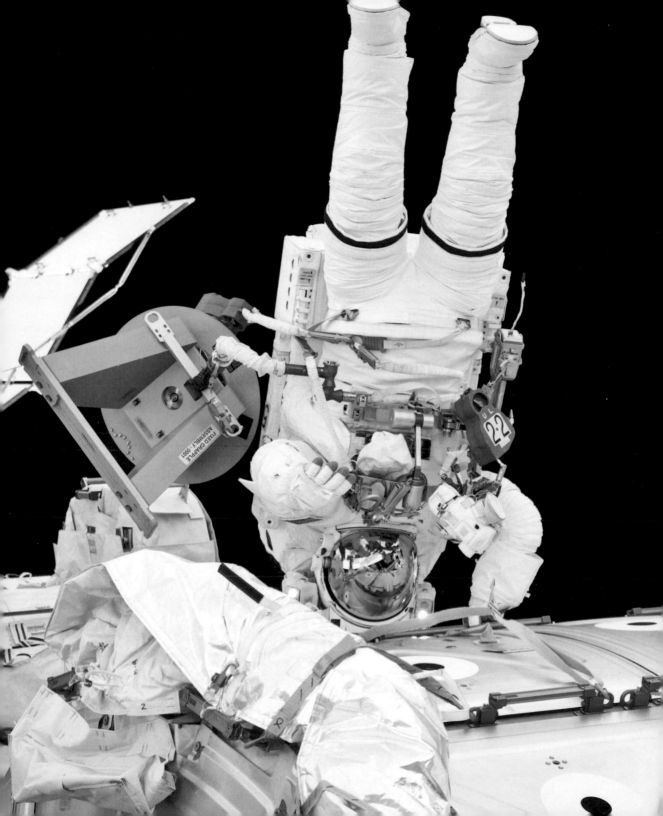

Astronaut Food

Astronauts eat food that is cooked on Earth and put into bags. People on Earth send food and water to the astronauts every few months. Turkey, nuts, tortillas, shrimp, and yogurt are some things an astronaut eats in space. There are ovens in the spaceships so astronauts can warm up their food.

Cosmic Fact

Astronauts often eat tortillas instead of bread because bread crumbles, and then the crumbs float around!

Staying Clean

In space, water is used only for drinking and preparing food. Water floats away, so there are no showers on spaceships. Astronauts use wet towels and hand wipes to stay clean. Also, astronauts cannot spit toothpaste into a sink, so they use a special kind that they can swallow. They can also spit it into a tissue.

Cosmic Fact

Toothpaste sticks to toothbrushes, so astronauts can brush their teeth upside down!

There are toilets on spaceships. To use one, an astronaut straps himself to the seat using a belt and toe straps. Waste is sucked into a tank because *everything* floats in space!

Cosmic Fact

Astronauts have to be trained how to use the special space toilets.

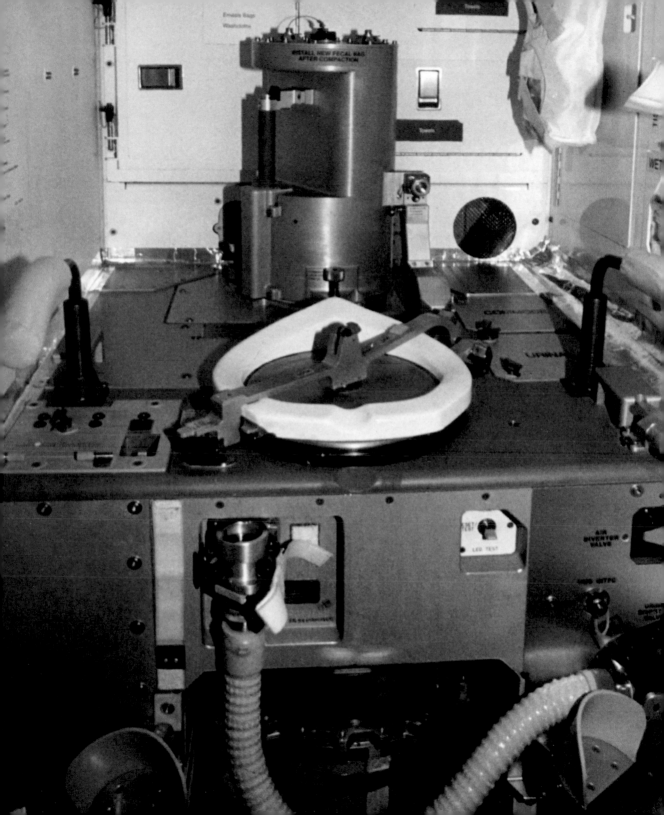

Fitness and Fun

Astronauts must exercise every day to keep their bodies strong. Floating does not use as many muscles as walking. Running on a treadmill is good exercise. Astronauts use straps to hold them down while they run.

Cosmic Fact

Doctors on Earth use computers to check on the astronauts' health while they are in space.

Astronauts work hard. But they have fun too! Doing flips in space is fun. So is playing with food. Astronauts toss candy or juice drops and try to catch them with their mouths. Some astronauts play musical instruments in space. They can even check their e-mail!

Cosmic Fact

Astronauts get video telephone calls from home every week. That way they can keep up with what is happening on Earth.

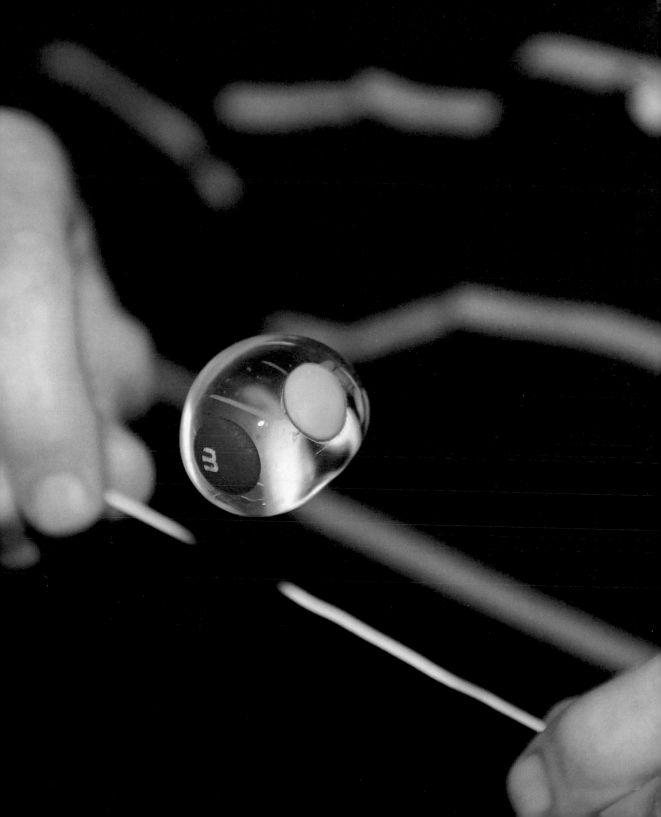

Sleeping Among the Stars

When it is time to sleep, most astronauts use sleeping bags. The sleeping bags are attached to a wall or chair. Astronauts often wear a mask over their eyes to block the light. Some astronauts listen to music before they fall asleep.

Cosmic Fact

It is not easy to know when to go to sleep in space. An astronaut in the space station would see 16 sunsets and sunrises every day!

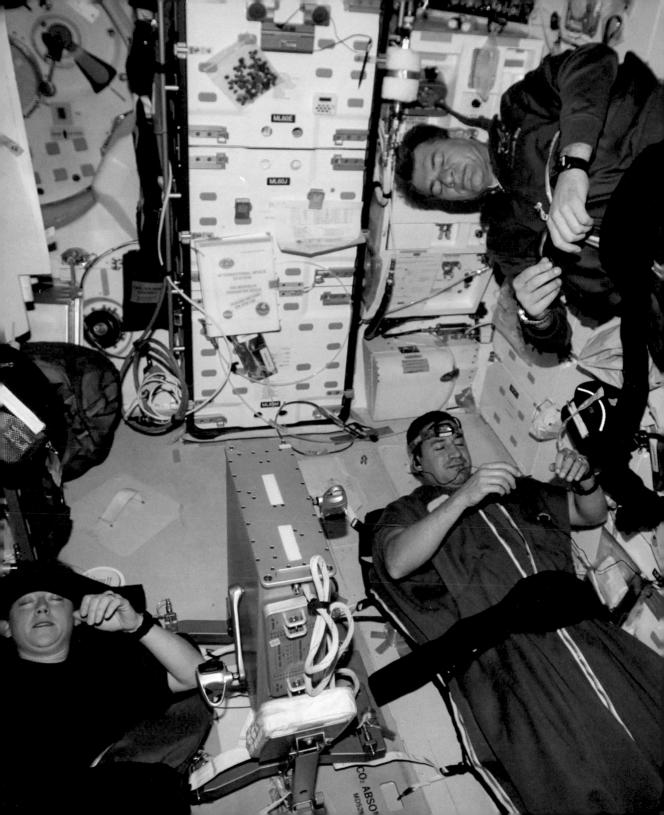

Becoming an Astronaut

Astronauts need a lot of training. First, they must finish college. Most astronauts study math, science, computers, or engineering. Pilots are trained to fly jet planes. Astronauts also need to be very healthy. They exercise and eat good food to keep their bodies strong.

Cosmic Fact

Floating in space is like floating in water. Astronauts practice for space walks in a giant swimming pool.

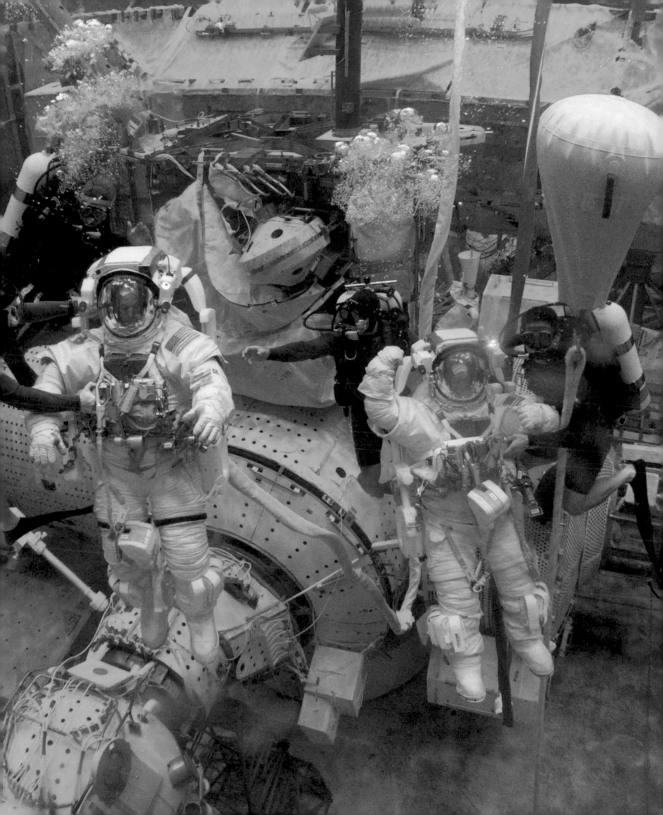

There are many jobs in space. Pilots fly spaceships. Doctors take care of the crew in space. Engineers keep the spaceships working. Biologists and chemists do experiments in space. Maybe someday you can become an astronaut and explore the galaxy too!

Cosmic Fact

Our galaxy is called the Milky Way. It is just one of the billions and billions of galaxies in the universe!

Learn More

Books

Kurkov, Lisa. *Blast! Into Space.* Greensboro, N.C.: Spectrum, 2014.

Lock, Deborah. *Astronaut: Living in Space.* New York: DK Children, 2013.

Wilson, Hannah. *Astronauts.* London: Kingfisher, 2015.

Web Sites

esa.int/esaKIDSen/LifeinSpace.html
Read what it is like to live in space. Also do fun puzzles and quizzes!

nasa.gov/audience/forkids/kidsclub/flash/
Learn about space, space travel, astronauts, and read stories by other kids.

Index

Published in 2016 by Enslow Publishing, LLC.
101 W. 23rd Street, Suite 240, New York, NY 10011

Copyright © 2016 by Carmen Bredeson

Enslow Publishing materials copyright © 2016 by Enslow Publishing, LLC.

Library of Congress Cataloging-in-Publication Data
Bredeson, Carmen, author.
 Astronauts explore the galaxy / Carmen Bredeson with Marianne Dyson.
   pages cm. — (Launch into space!)
 Summary: "Discusses what an astronaut is, what astronauts do, what life in space is like, and the training involved to become an astronaut"—Provided by publisher.
 Audience: Ages 8–10
 Audience: Grades 4 to 6
 Includes bibliographical references and index.
 ISBN 978-0-7660-6815-5 (library binding)
 ISBN 978-0-7660-6813-1 (pbk.)
 ISBN 978-0-7660-6814-8 (6-pack)
 1. Astronauts—Juvenile literature. 2. Astronauts—Training of—Juvenile literature. 3. Manned space flight—Juvenile literature. 4. Outer space—Exploration—Juvenile literature. I. Dyson, Marianne, author. II. Title.
 TL793.B7294 2015
 629.45—dc23

     2014050368

Printed in the United States of America

To Our Readers: We have done our best to make sure all Web site addresses in this book were active and appropriate when we went to press. However, the author and the publisher have no control over and assume no liability for the material available on those Web sites or on any Web sites they may link to. Any comments or suggestions can be sent by e-mail to customerservice@enslow.com.

Portions of this book originally appeared in the book *What Do Astronauts Do?*

Photo Credits: EpicStockMedia/Shutterstock.com (Cosmic Fact background); Milanares/iStock/Thinkstock (blue/green background throughout book); NASA, pp. 1 (astronaut); 3, 21, 23, 29; NASA/DVIDS, pp. 2 (all), 7, 9, 11, 13, 15, 17, 19, 25, 27; NASA/Victor Ivanov, p. 5; Zmiter/Shutterstock.com, p. 1 (rocket illustration).

Cover Credits: Milanares/iStock/Thinkstock (blue/green background); NASA (astronaut); Zmiter/Shutterstock.com (rocket illustration).